FAITH
and
MAJOR MENTAL ILLNESS

Stories, Meditations, and Essays

Marcia A. Murphy

RESOURCE *Publications* • Eugene, Oregon

FAITH AND MAJOR MENTAL ILLNESS
Stories, Meditations, and Essays

Copyright © 2025 Marcia A. Murphy. All rights reserved. Except for brief quotations in critical publications or reviews, no part of this book may be reproduced in any manner without prior written permission from the publisher. Write: Permissions, Wipf and Stock Publishers, 199 W. 8th Ave., Suite 3, Eugene, OR 97401.

Resource Publications
An Imprint of Wipf and Stock Publishers
199 W. 8th Ave., Suite 3
Eugene, OR 97401

www.wipfandstock.com

PAPERBACK ISBN: 979-8-3852-5385-2
HARDCOVER ISBN: 979-8-3852-5386-9
EBOOK ISBN: 979-8-3852-5387-6

Scripture quotations marked (ESV) are from The Holy Bible, English Standard Version (ESV), copyright ©2001 by Crossway Bibles, a publishing ministry of Good News Publishers. Used by permission. All rights reserved.

Scripture quotations marked (NIV) are taken from the Holy Bible, New International Version®, NIV®. Copyright © 1973, 1978, 1984, 2011 by Biblica, Inc.™ Used by permission of Zondervan. All rights reserved worldwide. www.zondervan.com. The "NIV" and "New International Version" are trademarks registered in the United States Patent and Trademark Office by Biblica, Inc.™

Scripture quotations marked (RSV) are from the Revised Standard Version of the Bible, copyright © 1946, 1952, and 1971 National Council of the Churches of Christ in the United States of America. Used by permission. All rights reserved worldwide.

This is dedicated to both—the Left and the Right

*What sculpture is to a block of marble,
education is to a human soul.*

– Joseph Addison

Contents

Preface ix

Acknowledgments xiii

Author's Note xiv

1 My Experience 1

2 Perspectives Matter 4

3 God's Answer to Prayer 6

4 Idolatry and Mental Health 11

5 Child Institutions 13

6 Stigma and the Church 17

7 Bible for Sanity 19

8 Housing 21

9 Thoughts about Work 27

10 Disability 28

11 On Being a Burden 31

12 Catholics and Protestants 32

13 Sidewalk 34

14 Stronghold 35

15 Resting in God 47

Appendix 53

Bibliography 55

Preface

IF YOU ARE LOOKING for entertainment you picked up the wrong book. This is not funny or amusing, or science fiction. This is about what touches my heart. Being emotionally blunted and numb, I can only write about things I do have some feelings about. Having psychosis, post-traumatic stress disorder (PTSD), and clinical depression for most of my life, I have often felt dead inside. Multiple traumatic experiences (both, physical and psychological), has partially deadened me. Mental afflictions can cause an emptiness inside of me. People sometimes remark about me: what a poker face, blunt affect—meaning my face shows no expression or little emotion. I don't laugh much. Sometimes, I might weep, but mostly in private. Otherwise, I usually have no passions and few feelings. And I won't let psychiatry get away with claiming they aren't partially to blame because the anti-psychotic medication I take can also have emotional numbness as a side-effect.

So any way you look at it, I'm a wounded human being. Looking for anything at all that can invoke feelings, I discovered religion is the biggest help. I do care about God. Considering what I've been through on earth it isn't difficult to imagine a real hell in the afterlife. And I don't want to go there. Religion in the form of Christianity has been comforting. But it provides more than a way out. Beyond this mess of human civilization full of bickering, strife, violence, and deception I believe there is a heavenly home, a dwelling full of love, joy, and peace. This is one of the few things I have feelings about. I care about my future and I care about anything in my present life that has to do with this. I don't have feelings about fashion, home décor, the lottery, or sports. I do have feelings about personal guilt, forgiveness, redemption, and eternal life. When I read the Judeo-Christian scriptures, I have feelings. It gives me hope and clarity. God is my advocate and vindicator. Few other people or things can do this. There are few other things that give me this assurance. Participating in a church worship service in a sanctuary gives me feelings. I sense the presence of God there. It is a feeling of profound peace and beauty.

I also feel injustice when things are not right. I do experience the emotion of compassion. I can see and feel it when the oppressed are being abused; especially when the poor or the weak are being afflicted with abuse. I can see what's wrong in the world and be angry. So, yes, anger is one of my emotions. I pray to God and ask for justice in this world. The Bible says that God will defend the downtrodden and oppressed. I have to have faith because, sometimes, wrongs will not be mended, I believe, until the afterlife. Sometimes people die at the hands of the oppressor; but God sees and hears everything. And in the end, God will make all things right. The oppressors will not win in the long run, and God's justice will prevail. This is the faith I have and my feelings.

I had a psychiatrist once, a long time ago. He passed away. He was a powerful resource for my feelings. This man had compassion. You see, I can feel it when I am valued, cared for, and loved. When people are kind to me, I have feelings. This psychiatrist was not a materialist. Yes, he had been educated to be a scientific doctor and he did research; but he went beyond this to become a holistic health care provider. There was more for him than that which met the eye. He was truly a doctor of the soul. His recognition of spiritual matters gave me hope and guidance. I did feel alive in his presence. I was not dead around him. I had feelings of hope. This psychiatrist brought healing.

> Psychiatry stands out among its medical counterparts in that to do the job well, you need to be able to go beyond the clinical aspects by being able to appreciate and understand the spiritual side in everyone. Being able to handle this sensitively and empathetically has

PREFACE

a significant potential impact upon the relationship between psychiatrist and patient, and therefore on the eventual treatment outcome.[1]

And there have been others. A few friends and occasionally, strangers. Usually, when I am with kind people I will feel alive. When I am around cruel, heartless people, I clam up and withdraw into myself. I get defensive. On the other hand, feeling God's love gives me freedom and courage. I have hope.

Sometime else which gives me some feelings is doing research through libraries. This may sound strange; however, it's true. There is something about looking for books and articles that gives me energy and joy. I often find joy in doing research. And when the librarians are helpful and kind, this is a joy. I don't seek information in general; but specifically, for certain topics or projects I pray about. This is related to my work, my mental health advocacy, and writing.

I do not understand how some people can live without God in a competitive, cutthroat, dog-eat-dog world, where anything goes. The world will tear you apart and wear you down. It can shorten your lifespan. I see my faith in Christ as the foundation of the truth, a bulwark of protection and support. I feel it is important to search for answers, including associating with God's people. To me, the alternative is insanity. Many people, when they turn their back on God, do become insane, literally, and all the while making life miserable for others.

In this book you can see how a dead person came to life through God, his word, religious worship, and fellowship with like-minded believers. The topic of this book, as I mentioned, is this: As a person who has felt so emotionally dead—which resulted from trauma, psychological deprivations, and major mental illness—what gives me any animation at all? How is religious faith involved and how can I experience emotions and purpose in life that will make me feel that life is worth living?

---

1. James, 2nd Edition Foreword: *Spirituality and Psychiatry*, xvii.

Acknowledgments

I GIVE MY THANKS to those who have given me a smile, a kind word or gesture to help me get through my day over the past several months. I also thank Matthew Wimer, managing editor of Wipf and Stock Publishers, for his patience and clear guidance, along with Joe Delahanty, marketing coordinator, and his staff for all their work, including the beautiful marketing flyers. I thank the excellent artistic cover designers, who over the years have created wonderful images. I am grateful to all of the people at Wipf and Stock Publishers for supporting my work. Thank you.

Author's Note

This is nonfiction.
The following stories and events are true
along with the accompanying information.

1

My Experience

I SUPPOSE I COULD begin this project by describing in technical terms what schizophrenia is; however, I would prefer to just let you know how my experience defined it. I had a psychotic break about the age of twenty-two, which means I had hallucinations which greatly disrupted my life. Before that I grew up in a home which had serious behavioral issues, one of which my younger brother tried to murder me. You can image my distress and the instability of my emotional life during this time period, finding no security, either in housing or with food needs. I became easy prey for a cult. Fast forward three and a half years to release from the evil group but then coming back home to where my younger brother now found me sexually attractive and I had to fight him off. Fortunately, I pushed him away and did not allow him to get very far. But the lack of protection, the neglect of protection from my parents and siblings, was additionally destabilizing and my emotional and psychological condition further deteriorated. All the while housing and food needs were still barely met and I was supposed to hold down employment which was obviously impossible.

Without the compassionate aid from a psychiatric professional who took me under his wing I would have soon disappeared into the deep, dark abyss. His assistance was the lifeline that gave me a way out of the mess of my biological family and the psychological distress that marked my first thirty years of life. As an adult, I developed relationships, some with males, that were in some ways helpful, and in other ways destructive. Post traumatic stress disorder (PTSD) haunted me, the condition of being stressed and upset, triggered, to the point of psychosis, due to memories of upsetting events. It often felt like there was no escape. Deep depression was in fluctuation with brief instances of hope and light. I turned to God in prayer and the thought of returning to my childhood faith of Christianity. Slowly, my life's direction obtained increasing stability and purpose.

Schizophrenia is not about split personalities or multiple personalities; those are different disorders. According to my psychiatrist, I have not been paranoid, nor delusional. I've experienced psychosis. The fallout has been familial, societal, and occupational. Stigma is a huge factor in lack of progress. Prejudice and ableism have hurt me numerous times. To put it quite frankly: people have hated me because I have a mental illness. This is devastating. I ask you to try to imagine what it feels like, the barriers to your ability to succeed. People can be so cruel and, unfortunately, the church is not exempt. Religious communities still have a way to go in growing in compassion for the mentally ill. Social inclusion is often elusive for someone with a psychiatric diagnosis. People need to see the whole person, not a psychiatric label. People with mental illness are human beings with feelings, needs, and wants. They want friendship like everybody else. They want friends who will talk to them, go out to lunch with them, and come over for coffee and chat.

I have been through extreme trauma, so much so, I beg the question: is recovery even possible? Will I ever feel liberated, free, and able to enjoy life? Will I ever have strong, stable relationships and be able to love again, fully, and without restraint? Can I overcome my condition called hypervigilance? Sleeping at night has been difficult since childhood. I am awake at all hours because I never feel safe and secure. Lately in my adult years there have been periodic times of rest, so it has improved. But I startle easily, jumping when hearing sudden noises, being constantly on guard. I am

My Experience

not paranoid, I have PTSD, and this is a feeling that danger is everywhere because in my past, it really *was*. My survival instinct is hypervigilant. Knowing that my life was in danger in the biological home setting programed me from an early age to be constantly on the alert. This is the primary way I know of to survive as an adult.

How does the process of coping with major mental illness influence my spiritual life? And, also, the reverse: How does faith influence my mental health condition? In this work I discuss a major mental illness—my own—and delve into whether recovery is possible from a personal perspective. As a person who was devastated by a psychotic disorder, post-traumatic stress disorder, and clinical depression, I take a look at prayer, scripture reading, and church life to see if these things have been contributing factors in building a healthier day-to-day existence, as I am afflicted with significant psychological and social challenges.

2

Perspectives Matter

> Breathe on me, breath of God,
> Fill me with life anew,
> That I may love what Thou dost love,
> And do what Thou wouldst do.
>
> EDWIN HATCH, 1878

SINCE MY FORTIES my prayer has been to love what God loves, and to do what God would do. These lyrics through prayer transformed my life. Many days as I passed a homeless man on the street and handed him a dollar or some change, our love for one another eventually grew to where he is now a prominent person in my life, a companion and dear friend. God put it into my heart to love and serve him as Christ would do. By Christ living in me it became possible to have compassion on someone who was cast out of society, whom most people hated, and who was left outside to die.

You see, winters in my part of the United States are bitter and cold, with windchills reaching negative 60° Fahrenheit. Homeless people die every year around here, the upper Midwest. To ignore this fact reveals how callous human hearts can be and how an unwillingness to produce change will become fatal for victims of the cold winters. So, one night, Christmas Eve to be exact, I took steps to find him housing.

I mention this situation not to boast but to illustrate how God transformed me: once, a selfish, self-centered, bikini-clad-sun worshipper, and tennis fanatic, into a human being that felt concern for the well-being of those who suffer. How as a naïve and foolish young person I was transformed over time through Bible study and religious worship into a new, caring persona which is more of a reflection of Jesus Christ. God changes lives; he really does. And in my case, it wasn't just a change for me, but also for the benefit of others.

Being malnourished for most of my adult life due to extreme subsistence-level poverty, my vitamin deficiencies contributed to sick mental health. Irritability, anger, impulsiveness, you name it, my personality flaws seemed to be beyond my immediate control. And this often got me into trouble. Not jail time, mind you; but problems within various relationships. I've been married twice. And divorced twice. And the man I'm with now is not my husband. Sort of like the woman at the well (John 4:1–42 RSV). I can assure you, I'm no saint; but I'm teachable and that's what counts. I do believe that God provided the partner I now have to help me with my physical and mobility needs, issues due to multiple disabilities. He also cares for me spiritually. In addition, the fact that my remaining time on earth is limited with, perhaps, only ten to twenty years or so left, convinces me to think a little harder and deeper: *How can I use my remaining years for God's glory?*

Prayer continues to be paramount, seeking God's guidance. To aid in my thinking and seeking clarity for ideas I felt like asking some church friends what their perspectives were on prayer and what their own relationships with God were like. I used questionnaires and these respondents illustrate the manifold perspectives of how God intervenes in our lives; and, perhaps, this gives us hope for ourselves, our own faith development.

3

God's Answer to Prayer

HEARING HOW GOD IS active in the lives of my friends helps to strengthen my own faith. Here is an example from a senior person of my church. I asked her how God answered her prayers.

Marcia: Jan, please describe why you decided to turn to God in prayer.

Jan: My husband died after fighting bladder cancer for three years. During that time, we had prayed for a cure, followed every doctor and specialists' recommendations, and searched medical libraries for studies regarding dietary changes that might help cure cancer. Despite years of morning and nightly prayers that his life be spared, he succumbed to the cancer in December of 1993. My immediate question was, "Why, God?" But knowing that some answers to our whys must wait until we, too, are in heaven, I changed my prayer to, "God, what do I do with the rest of my life? I'm only fifty-three years old and have a long time ahead of me. I don't feel like living. What will make it worthwhile?"

Marcia: Did you perceive an answer to your prayer right away?

Jan: God didn't answer immediately, but I kept asking. During Lent several churches joined to serve a luncheon and a brief service each Thursday. I joined a friend who also worked at the University to walk to the Catholic Church holding that year's

Lenten luncheons. On our walk, she mentioned that her church was going to build a Habitat for Humanity home for a family who would be unable to buy their own home without help. This had been made possible through a bequest in a woman's will of $15,000 to be matched by the church membership, making the $30,000 that was at that time needed to build a Habitat home with lots of help from volunteers. That interested me a lot and I asked if she would invite me to go help on one of the workdays.

As I got home and thought more about it, I said to myself, I wish I could do that. I think my church could raise matching funds to build a house. I said to myself, "I wish I had $15,000. I don't think I prayed it, just wished it.

Marcia: It appears that God's answer to your prayer was rather complex. Please describe more of your experience.

Jan: About the same time that all of this was happening I was meeting with a financial consultant to invest my husband's life insurance and retirement money. The consultant was going to invest the money in funds that would grow. He suggested that we meet every three months to see how the money invested was increasing, and how I might want to change the funds' allocations. Three months later when I saw him again, he said, "Your investments have done very well this quarter. They have grown, by $17,000."

My heart almost stopped: $17,000! That was more than the $15,000 I had sort of wished for. Thoughts raced through my head. Should I go home and think about it? No! God had given me my answer, so I said to the consultant: "This is not what you are expecting to hear from me, but I want you to take $15,000 of the increase to the pastor of my church and donate it anonymously to be matched to build a Habitat for Humanity house. This is what he did. I must admit that I worked very hard (anonymously) to get church members to raise that additional money. I spoke to women's missionary circles, Sunday School classes, made announcements at church services, even had the children's Sunday School classes design a t-shirt pattern that all our church volunteer workers would wear.

Marcia: It looks like everything worked out well. Please continue.

Jan: Yes, a year later, we were ready to build a house. But a serendipity bonus, while my $15,000 waited in an interest-earning fund where the minister had placed it and monthly added the matching funds that the church raised, it had grown and now totaled $40,000, enough for one third of another house!

Marcia: That's incredible! Did other people get involved?

Jan: Almost everyone in our church got involved. Some came in work clothes with hammers, hardhats, and ladders. Others brought food for the workers. One lady babysat the family's disabled daughter in a trailer someone donated to be put on the site. Habitat had built houses in a week, so we planned groundbreaking on one Sunday, with the dedication of the house and turnover of the keys to the new homeowners the next Sunday. That was a little ambitious, and I don't think our habitat chapter has ever attempted another one-week build. We even had to borrow fans to be brought in to dry the walls when we had very humid days.

Many church members continued to volunteer with Habitat for years. Two even worked in Habitat's office for a time. I served on their Board of Directors and continued to help build houses for ten years. Of the first twenty-five houses our Habitat chapter built, I worked on twenty-three of them. I had asked God what to do with the rest of my life; he surely came through on that one! [End of Jan]

The following response to my survey comes from a young woman named Sara who is very involved with the church I attend and who is also a wife and mother.

Sara said: I write in a prayer journal each night. I pray for: healing, guidance, protection, strength, and leading. Also, I usually ask God for safety, relationship and health-related concerns for my family, friends and myself, and sometimes social justice and health and safety issues for those around the world suffering from war, natural disasters, disease, and famine. I also ask for forgiveness (maybe this falls under "provision"?). I include a list of things for which I am grateful. Or I go back and review previous entries and thank God for answered prayers.

Marcia: Can you give an example of an answered prayer?

Sara: After our first-born child died from Severe Combined Immunodeficiency (SCID) we decided to have more children despite their risk of inheriting the same disorder as their older sister. The first time was an easier choice than the second time because if our youngest had been born with the disorder it would have meant many months away from our second-born because of the treatment and recovery process of someone born with SCID. We prayed incessantly for healthy children. Each time we received word they were healthy and without SCID it was a clear and obvious answer to prayers and two of the best days of my life!

Sara continues: Another example of answered prayer was when we decided to raise a service dog in training for someone with PTSD, we didn't really know what to expect. Bear is a *huge*, sometimes loud, and sometimes reactive, black German Shepherd who we never felt would be a fit for our family should he fail as a service dog. However, he is a sweet, smart dog who, unfortunately, had some of this own PTSD, so we wanted to give him the best shot to live his best life with the person/family who needed him. Even though we only signed up to raise him for a few months, we ended up having him in our home for fifteen months! In that time we worked with him, trained him, and loved on him. The whole time I was anxious he wouldn't find his match with a person/veteran who has PTSD, and that we would feel obligated to keep him. I prayed every day he would find a match or that we would be the right family for him. When the trainer called and said she had found the *perfect* match (a man without injuries who could handle a powerful dog like Bear, and one who even used to have a black German Shepherd name Bear), it seemed like it could only be a *God thing*. It just felt right. [End of Sara]

Pat is a senior church friend who responded to my survey. She shared her experience also.

Marcia: Pat, please explain your experience with God and prayers.

Pat: I hope when I pray to receive guidance and strength. I do not expect God to give me things I ask want, even healing. When our granddaughter, Samantha, was finally sent to the ICU it was during a prayer service on video from Jeremy and Sara's [the parents] home church. The church was having a prayer meeting in Stillwater, Oklahoma, and Jeremy and Sara were in the Children's Hospital in Cincinnati watching on the video. So, many people were praying and at that same instant she started to fail even more.

Did God answer all those prayers? No, [not in the way we wanted]. However, we do know of at least one baby who lived because of Samantha. Were all our prayers answered the way we wanted, no. But we did receive strength to keep going and guidance to help others. Since then Jeremy and Sara [the parents] have been very active in new born screening and the Immune Deficiency Foundation. Later they were brave enough to have two more children who did not have the genetic disease SCID. God did answer, with no when we wanted yes, but we have come to understand that many lives have been saved because of Jeremy and Sara working hard to have new born screening for SCID. When Samantha was born, only eight states had screening; now all of them do! Her pediatrician told us in the funeral receiving line that she had spotted one potential patient with similar symptoms. Many pediatricians never see a SCID patient, a rare disease. And, the pediatrician's patient is now cured of SCID! Prayer answered but not my way, but *God's*. [End of Pat]

4

Idolatry and Mental Health

WHEN SOMETHING TAKES THE PLACE OF GOD

WORSHIPPING IDOLS MAKES A person mentally ill. When something is taking the place of God in a person's life, mental illness develops in that person. No one is exempt. Throughout all of history we see God working to restore the human race to their rightful place as children of God. Many people think that their career is the most important thing to them. However, in the end, it will fail to fulfill either by the supervisor's betrayal or your own burnout. Nothing can fulfill us more than having a right relationship with the Almighty, our creator. The one who created us wants to have our full attention, wants us to focus. Then all the rest in our lives will fall into place.

Many psychiatric patients put all their focus and trust in the therapist; however, if the therapist becomes more important than God and, in addition, the therapist's advice is unbiblical, the therapeutic relationship will turn sour and disappoint. Because no human being, however wise, can take the place of God.

And the same is true with our spouse. Marriage can be a blessing; but when it is the highest priority, it will sour and fail us. As is true with the family unit. Putting relatives i.e., parents, siblings, or children above God is idolatry. Children cannot always have their own way. Parents need to guide them using biblical principles.

How can we prioritize God? By keeping his commandments, to love him with our whole heart, mind, soul, and strength; and to love our neighbors as ourselves. *"Love the Lord your God with all your heart and with all your soul and with all your mind and with all your strength. The second is this: 'Love your neighbor as yourself.' There is no commandment greater than these."* (Mark 12: 30–31 NIV)

5

Child Institutions

I TOUCHED UPON WHY I sometimes feel emotionally dead earlier in the Preface. Here are additional thoughts on the topic. First and, foremost, I will state that early childhood upbringing, does, indeed, influence how we will develop psychologically. I know there are people who state our life is all about choices we make, the good choices and the bad; however, our family environments, the social interactions within the family as we grow up do play a tremendous part in how we will develop. The way we are treated, our role models, our authorities, those who raise us and teach in our schools, do play an important part in our feelings about ourselves and the outer world. Our mindsets, our emotions, our mental states are tremendously shaped (or you could say, influenced) by childhood experiences within the home and educational systems.

And so I say with conviction that I do feel a strong affinity with the widely publicized Romanian orphan babies who were institutionalized in the 1900s. These babies where warehoused and provided with only physical requirements for survival without other human interaction or contact. Such deprivation resulted in either early death or severe mental and emotional developmental delays or permanent damage.[1] I feel a deep connection. The studies of these children show that without close emotional and

---

1. Simms, "Intimacy and Institutionalization," 81–86.

psychological bonding in infancy, these babies died or if they survived, had severe mental and emotional disabilities. They could not grow psychologically and, also, suffered mental retardation. I may not have mental retardation, but I do have significant emotional maladjustments often by feeling dead inside. My intellect is only capable of a narrow area of functioning. Though scoring high on IQ tests, I still would not be capable of a college degree because of my narrow focus and ability in only certain topics.

My mother was distracted with my two older siblings close to me in age so I got little one-on-one time with her. No matter how many siblings, those mothers who treat each child as special will convey to each child that they are cherished even if time spent with them is limited. But this doesn't always happen; it depends on the heart of the mother and the specific way she treats each individual child. Also, I was not breast fed so I lacked the closeness and emotional bonding from breast feeding. I did receive some kind of food and was an overweight baby, child, and teen. Babies who are not breast fed usually develop obesity later on in life.

My mother was largely nonverbal. She rarely spoke. I cannot remember my mother speaking to me unless she was angry about something. I had little interactions with my father, but some, I remember, were abusive. Since I suffered from an environmental lack of stimulation like the Romanian babies, I developed an inner world of my own, sometimes even hearing imaginary voices in the attic.

As a baby I did not receive much hugging or affection. And as I grew older, my mother continued to be emotionally cold. If I ever tried to hug her she would stiffen her body, making a growling sound indicating hostility. I remember my maternal grandmother striking me in anger because I was "slow." My siblings hated me and tormented me by bullying and my parents did not intervene to stop them. My father occasionally tried to provide warmth but it got perverted and the rest of my life I felt uncomfortable around him. So, I not only had problems with my younger brother but, also, with my dad. This caused a great deal of psychological damage and distress.

CHILD INSTITUTIONS

I went through my entire infancy and childhood without receiving much affection or healthy emotional intimacy. That is why going to school was such a rewarding experience, because I remember my female elementary school teachers as giving me attention and showing an interest in me. I loved school because that is where I experienced psychological warmth. Because of my lack of intimacy with my biological mother, I was unable to form good, healthy attachments as I grew up. The school teachers helped somewhat and temporarily filled that gap because they seemed to care about me. I could only survive because of my experience in the public school system. Without the schools I never would have made it. Even to this day I love libraries, books, and education.

As a teen and adult, I tried to obtain love from girlfriends or boyfriends, but not with much luck. I did seek heterosexual relationships, but the men were abusive. It was not until I achieved some social integration within the Christian community that I developed some good, healthy relationships with women and men. I am still learning, even now, how to form healthy attachments.

All of this is why I still have residual emotional problems of feeling dead inside. And in contrast, I can have problems with the strong emotion of anger. I sometimes cannot contain my anger and I will have an outburst, sometimes with swear words. I have prayed about this for a long time and I can see prayer does help. My childhood upbringing is also one reason I have blunted affect (not much facial expression). My emotional development is blunted. When a kind, supportive psychiatrist started therapy with me for psychiatric illness as an adult, I was still emotionally immature. I was naïve and trusting. I believed whatever people told me and was, subsequently, harmed. This psychiatrist helped me to grow up and mature somewhat in a safe therapeutic relationship.

There are people who mock me because of how my face looks and they also mock me for saying few words, or not talking much. Some people are very uncomfortable because I don't say much. But they don't understand. I just don't have the energy to speak, it is too difficult. I'm usually not strong enough to use my voice. People accuse me of wrong doing all because I am quiet. They don't like quiet people. They think all people should be gregarious, loud, and talkative. Such ignorance. I have a right to not speak. I am not being rude. I have a right to be quiet. I will communicate the best I can and writing is one way I communicate well (or so I am told).

Another thing that I have strong feelings about is that I was not intended to have children. That was not my mission in life. I have no regrets regarding children. My mission was to study truth, beauty, and love, and to write about important matters related to psychology, psychiatry, and religion, the way these are intertwined. My mission was and continues to be about how faith, spirituality, and mental health are related. I could have been something other than a writer, but God wanted me to engage with the culture and explore the world of the mentally ill. I was to be engaged with survival issues and learn how the poor struggle to survive while dealing with a mental illness. I was also to seek and implement solutions.

Because of my encounter with God in my early life I have had the mission to share my faith with others. And since I've experienced mental illness, my role was in this area of society. I believe that knowing Christ is the key to recovery in all parts of life for the mentally ill. I am not a pluralist. I don't believe that all religions are equally valid because it is logically impossible due to contradictions in their theological concepts and meaning. Pluralism is a dogma all its own which is just as exclusive as any other single religious belief. I believe there is a right way and a wrong way, an objective truth. Some things are true and other things are false, not subjective, or relative. People need to open their hearts to the one Triune God who draws all people into a loving relationship with him through Christ. My sanity is based on this truth. I've experienced extreme mental illness and the rest of this book will help explain why I believe as I do.

6

Stigma and the Church

I WAS DOWN ON my knees facing the east window where soon I'd see the sunrise for another sabbath day. A Sunday of worship. But I didn't want to go again to this church, a church where I felt rejected and ridiculed. And so I prayed—begged—on my knees "Lord God, *please*, I don't want to go there. Please don't make me."

This happened on numerous occasions over a period of years. And eventually, my faith drained away, so much so that my writing entered the phase of proving to myself that Christianity was, indeed, true. Afterall, Jesus was my savior. However, the church, the formal institution . . .

Many times, I thought, *I had more faith before I got involved in a church.* There were micro-aggressive social interactions where the church members used tone of voice as a weapon to put me down. There was even one area in the church building that I named, the Bermuda Triangle, where most abuse occurred regularly. I then tried to avoid that area.

I would go to church looking for the love of God; and, instead, the wicked attacks by harsh tones of voice let me know that I was not accepted. I was not welcome there at all. Such crushing experiences threw me into despair because I could not find the love of God. The people hated me—some of them anyway—and they let me know it.

So my ideas for writing eventually began to focus on how could I keep my faith, when I told God on several occasions that I was losing my faith. Sure, others had faith; but I was losing mine. Maybe my newest book would be about how I lost my faith.

God will use other resources to get his love to us. So then, love came mostly from the civic sector. Many of the city bus drivers, in particular, became a source of God's love and care, the way they were so very respectful and kind, with caring tones of voice. Often the librarians in the public libraries, or certain staff in hospitals would treat me well. God still wanted to reach me with his love.

Hopefully, the church is coming around. God is having me avoid certain situations at church. And I have an advocate now, so this helps. This is new. I have a strong male partner, who has both, strong character, and who is physically strong. He loves me and we go everywhere together. He sticks up for me and when he is with me, people give me more space and respect. Sometimes, at home, I let him do all the praying. He says that God loves us. And he loves God. Sometimes, my partner's faith was all I had. I needed to regain my own. And forgive.

Many Sunday mornings I would pray for the strength to love my enemies, to go to this place of worship and love and forgive my enemies as Christ taught. How strange to feel this way at God's house, to not feel or be safe, but on guard. So, I trudge on. I keep trying to have faith realizing that God's house has both good and bad people, and God will judge them, not me. Sometimes I feel we are all in transition and being made new, both good and bad people, being transformed over time. And God will vindicate me, defend me. "Let not your hearts be troubled. Believe in God; believe also in me." (John 14:1 ESV)

7

Bible for Sanity

THE HOLY BIBLE SAYS that God is good. The enemy of God wants us to think otherwise. When I see the news on-line it has sometimes shaken my faith. So much destruction, violence, obscenities, you name it. Things contrary to God and his beauty, truth, and love. The world can throw a lot at you. It slings mud. Then we wash it off with our spiritual showering at Sunday morning worship, attending the church service that makes us clean, purified, and new again. We find Christ where two or three are gathered in his name. "For where two or three are gathered in my name, there am I in the midst of them." (Matt 18:20 RSV)

I would be totally lost without the Bible; the words of scripture have great power. In the Bible, specifically, the book of Psalms, we can see God's great love and mercy, his compassion for *us*. Sure, the news report has a lot of bad things, but go back to the Bible. This will save your sanity. For the world is a mad place but we have to live in it, coping.

Reading the Bible every day changes my brain. I go from muddled, and foggy, to clear, logical, and strong. The words of scripture change the structure of what my biological brain is composed of. I can feel it and experience it with the transformation of my mind. Not only this, but I receive clarity of values and purpose.

Faith and Major Mental Illness

I gain commitment. I gain hope for the new day. I gain a sense of faith and belief in the God who does answer prayer. I've seen my prayers answered.

8

Housing

FOR MANY YEARS I have had to live in substandard housing. To help you understand what I mean I will give a description: The plumbing became an issue for example. The kitchen sink pipes would back up and run all over the floor. This needed to be repaired several times. Once a girlfriend from church came and fixed it. She renovated houses, cabins, and apartments all the time though her weekend hobby, and is a university professor.

The bathroom sink pipes also got plugged often and after being temporarily cleared, would get plugged up again soon after. The landlord didn't want to fix it anymore. The city sewer repair man told me it wasn't my fault, that the problem was much farther down. Same thing with my bathtub pipe, it got clogged on a regular basis and I was told the problem was much deeper than my apartment. If I had lacked the repairmen's support, the landlord would have charged me hundreds of dollars for repairs. I didn't have any extra money for repairs though, as I was visiting the crisis center food pantry because of my personal food scarcity and insecurity. I barely could survive on what income I had. I lived at a subsistence level. A dear church friend offered to save me from this dilemma with financial support for plumbing repairs; but when the repairmen told the landlord it wasn't my fault I did not need my friend's assistance.

The electric stove's oven didn't work. When I asked the landlord for assistance, they put in a new stove but it was so cheap its oven didn't work either. Then they sent a repair man, but he didn't fix it. So I basically went about twenty years without being able to bake anything. My church supported me by purchasing a microwave oven, so that helped, and I could still use a couple of burners on the stove-top.

I had to brush my teeth at the kitchen sink because of the clogged sink pipe in the bathroom. If water was run there out of the faucet a friend would use a cup and scoop the accumulated water out of the sink and into a bucket. Then he would carry the bucket to the kitchen sink and dump out the dirty water. A neighbor, when she heard about this, told me it wasn't sanitary.

Then, there were mice. I didn't see the mice until after living about nineteen years in this apartment; but soon after spotting them I was able to move out. However, the mice were not the main reason for moving out. There were multiple factors, some of which I mentioned previously. In addition to all this the next-door neighbors seemed to think it was their purpose in life to torment me. There was a man in the apartment across the hall and he liked to walk around completely naked in the building hallway late at night. He told me he was spying on my computer activities through his own computer. His mouth was a well-spring (or should I say sick-spring) of profanities and furious anger. He would yell at the mailman, he yelled at the people living in the units next to, and below him. He yelled at everybody, myself included. He had a vegetable garden out back and grew tomatoes. He told me to help myself any time to the produce; however, when I did this one day he cursed me from out of his second-story window: -#**>#//! What are you *doing*, Marcia?!"

This man and also a female neighbor who harassed me made my life hell and as a consequence my religious faith faltered. It became apparent that bullying behaviors had been normalized in their childhood upbringing so they felt they were absolutely free to inflict emotional, psychological, and physical harm on others. And the police wouldn't help. And the landlord said his hands were tied since the police wouldn't intervene first.

The Bible says do not seek revenge, but leave it to the wrath of God. We are to love and feed our enemy:

> Bless those who persecute you; bless and do not curse them. Rejoice with those who rejoice, weep with those who weep. Live in harmony with one another; do not be haughty, but associate with the lowly; never be conceited. Repay no one evil for evil, but take thought for what is noble in the sight of all. If possible, so far as it depends upon you, live peaceably with all. Beloved, never avenge yourselves, but leave it to the wrath of God; for it is written, "Vengeance is mine, I will repay, says the Lord." No, "if your enemy is hungry, feed him; if he is thirsty, give him drink; for by so doing you will heap burning coals upon his head." Do not be overcome by evil, but overcome evil with good. (Rom 12:14–21 RSV)

So I prayed daily for my neighbors. I asked God to help them with their needs. I asked God to bless them. One day, I offered a brand new gallon of milk to my female neighbor by knocking on her door and holding it out to her, asking if she'd like it. She screwed up her face as though the milk were poison; she shook her head, no, then abruptly slammed the door shut. On another occasion I put a peace offering at the foot of her door consisting of a decorative bag with a grocery gift card with a small box of chocolate candies. She seemed happy with that, thanking me in the hallway. But after a few weeks, the abuse resumed. She seemed totally obsessed with harassing me and it seemed demonic. She drew a large black line on my apartment door with a marker. On several occasions, she would put black marker ink in my apartment door's security peep hole so I couldn't see who was standing outside my door. She also put Super-glue into my mail box key hole and tore off my name tag on the box. This is a federal crime and for a while I couldn't get my mail until it was fixed. Even though a postal supervisor said my neighbor committed a felony, she never got prosecuted. To hear more of the details of the abuse I endured over a number of years see my previous publication, *Knitting with Barbed Wire*.[1]

The air conditioning in my apartment was an issue as well. The summer temperatures with high humidity in Iowa go sometimes above ninety or above one hundred degrees, especially the heat index. The heat build-up in my second-floor apartment became life-threatening. Also, my body has a medical condition called heat intolerance or body heat regulation disorder. My body cannot regulate itself with the heat or cold temperatures well. This is partially the result of a psychiatric medication I am on and, also, another unrelated medical disorder. In addition, my medications were ruined by the extreme heat on more than one occasion. It was difficult to get my insurance to pay for the extra new prescriptions/refills, so sometimes, I had to pay the cost out of pocket.

When my A/C broke down (a wall unit) the heat went way above 100 degrees in my apartment and on several occasions, I nearly had a heat stroke. One day, I nearly died. A good friend saved my life by walking ten minutes in the extreme heat to a near-by grocery store to purchase a large bag of ice cubes. He then brought it to me and I applied ice packs in cloths to every part of my head, face, and body. This friend literally saved my life, my physician affirmed. My face got very red, I felt awful, and I almost died. Additionally, this friend found all the electric fans in my apartment and hooked them up in my room and turned them full-force on me, neglecting himself in the process. This friend sacrificed himself for my benefit. He is Roman Catholic in upbringing.

The next day, gratefully, at my request, the landlord had the maintenance man install a new A/C unit and that helped enormously. However, these A/C units usually gave out within three years and so this emergency situation was recurring every few years. I never knew when it would happen next. I didn't feel safe.

I also was not safe in going out to stand at the bus stop to catch the bus. I prayed for protection. The neighborhood was known for stalkers, many of whom had just been released from prison or who drove into town from the surrounding rural areas.

---

1. Murphy, *Knitting Barbed Wire*, 36–37.

Housing

One stalker lived in the apartment below me—again, the police did nothing when I asked for help. The pickup trucks and vans going up and down the streets in the early morning hours had stalkers who loved to see who was walking outside or waiting at a bus stop. They also liked to watch the swimmers go into the building that had the pool a couple of blocks away. One such truck pulled up beside me as I walked to the pool to work out and he stopped. I had a stare-down with the driver and walked away.

People just released from prison had the opportunity for housing in a nearby complex that did not do background checks for potential clients. Of course, this is a great blessing for those needing second chances; however, on the other hand some of these people have emotional problems and do not know how to act in a civilized manner with the resulting yelling, fights, violence, and illegal activities like drug-dealing and prostitution. Most days, if I wanted my windows open for fresh air, I had to endure listening to profanity being loudly tossed out like used garbage.

I never could afford a vacuum cleaner, so a dear church friend came over a few times a year with hers and did the job of vacuuming. I managed to scrub the hard floors, but later got help from my home health aide. The apartment had an old-fashioned refrigerator and the freezer part frosted and iced-up periodically. It was very difficult to clean out this frost and thick ice. It would soon accumulate and I would chip away at the layers. Once a large block of ice slid out and crashed down on top of my foot.

Because my apartment was on a second floor my friend, and personal care attendant (who doubled as home health aide), would have to carry my heavy wheelchair up and down the stairs. Fortunately, my apartment manager had compassion and supported my move to a better apartment that would be disability accessible. I was able to move to a place that had an elevator. This new apartment was a major upgrade and tremendous improvement in my living conditions.

The apartment I moved to had new flooring of vinyl planks the color of beautiful natural blond wood. The walls were freshly painted with a lovely white hue. Everything was sparkling clean and all the appliances worked. The neighbors seem pleasant and cordial. This is certainly a touch of Heaven.

The only way this move was possible was because church friends helped. There were two mini-vans, an SUV, and another car with seven friends helping to load everything up and transport my belongings across town and into my new place. One even shed his blood, as I saw blood stains on a chest of drawers. These are Christian people. They believe in helping out. We did it all in one trip. Priar to the move some additional church friends supplied moving boxes.

Now I live in a wonderful place that is in a good location i.e., close to the city's public library, restaurants, and stores that are helpful and pleasant to visit. The view from my sixth-floor apartment window is spectacular, a cityscape, along with trees, birds, and airplanes flying by. It lets in abundant sunshine as well.

I'm grateful to God for all his goodness to me, his faithfulness. Though it took many years to move to a nice new home, God, in his mercy, heard my cries for deliverance from my enemies, and answered me. The Christian people are God's people. When I needed assistance in moving to a new apartment, they came to my aid. Without them, I never could have done it. God provided what I needed. I thank God.

9

Thoughts About Work

SOMEONE SAID I DO my research and writing because it provides me a sense of achievement and accomplishment. What he said about these things may have some truth; but it is only a partial truth.

My motivation to write is not solely to accomplish something. I write because I believe what I have to say has some intrinsic and inherent value. What I say is to make a difference in someone's life, change lives, even my own.

Doctor Russell Noyes Jr., my former psychiatrist who retired and then passed away, valued what I said in my writing. He thought what I had to say was important. I never started writing to accomplish anything except, perhaps, to communicate a message. My motivation is more than simply work; it has intrinsic value. To solely work to accomplish something is superficial and shallow, and will not feel fulfilling. Spiritual meaning cannot be found in external achievements. If so, then the man rolling the stone up the hill only to find it falling back down again, would be happy because he could just roll the stone back up the hill again, and then it falls, and he pushes it up again, and it goes on and on like this for eternity. But we cannot find happiness in rolling the stone up the hill repeatedly, endlessly. This is emptiness.

Work has to have meaning, spiritual meaning. There must be a reason deeper than achievement.

10

Disability

BEGINNING IN MY FIFTIES both of my lower limbs became progressively disabled through an increase in pain, and weakness. The chronic pain was and is, currently, severe. There are some Christians who think that physical illness and disease is a result of a sinful life. However, Christ was sympathetic and compassionate and healed the sick and lame; and in doing so, he usually didn't accuse them of any wrong doing. In my own experience I have found that confession of known sins did not bring about physical healing. I have prayed to God on numerous occasions, daily, repenting for everything I can think of and even things I'm not aware of doing. I tried to leave nothing out. But, still, no relief. I have prayed for healing, relief from pain, and for strength. These prayers have gone unanswered or perhaps there is a reason for my disability which may result in a spiritual healing.

Joni Eareckson Tada is an American Christian author, radio host, artist, and founder of Joni and Friends, an organization of Christian ministry in the disability community. Currently in her mid-seventies, she became paralyzed from a diving accident when she was seventeen years old and has needed a wheelchair ever since her accident. In her many books and talks, she shares about her experience of praying to God on numerous occasions, asking for healing and the ability to walk again. But she has never regained this ability. She has expressed that she came to know and depend on Jesus Christ through her ordeal and has been spiritually changed for the better because of her disability.

I want to incorporate this wisdom into my own life. Both, my mental disability, and physical disability has forced me to rely on God for my every need. It has been a means of transformation, though I still have a long way to go. I am learning patience, kindness, humility, and hopefully, more generosity toward others. I seek wisdom and a biblical understanding of God and his ways. Things are different now that I use a wheelchair part of the time along with being part-time on forearm crutches. I have a different perspective. I trust that God will provide. My personal care assistant (PCA) is a strong individual, physically, as well in character and faith. We pray together two to three times a day. And he uses the sign of the cross. I have been learning the skills of friendship and that a companion in my disability is a great blessing. I have learned that God can still use me for his purposes. As a writer and advocate for the mentally and physically disabled, the world can hear from the oppressed and downtrodden, those marginalized, the outcasts. I try to share how we feel and see the world; but most importantly, how we experience the presence of God. I share our pain and joys, our concerns, and trials. I let the world know that though weak, in Christ, we are strong. The Lord [Jesus Christ] said to the Apostle Paul: "My grace is sufficient for you, for my power is made perfect in weakness." And Paul said: "I will all the more gladly boast of my weaknesses, that the power of Christ may rest upon me. For the sake of Christ, then, I am content with weaknesses, insults, hardships, persecutions, and calamities; for when I am weak, then I am strong" (2 Cor 12:9–10 RSV).

The Bible also says that a blind man was not sinful in the sense that this had caused his blindness: As he [Jesus Christ] went along, he saw a man blind from birth. His disciples asked him, "Rabbi, who sinned, this man or his parents, that he was born blind?"

"Neither this man nor his parents sinned," said Jesus, "but this happened so that the works of God might be displayed in him. As long as it is day, we must do the works of him who sent me. Night is coming, when no one can work. While I am in the world, I am the light of the world."

After saying this, he spit on the ground, made some mud with the saliva, and put it on the man's eyes. "Go," he told him, "wash in the Pool of Siloam" (this word means *Sent*). So the man went and washed, and came home seeing (John 9: 1–7 NIV).

11

On Being a Burden

My good friend, Opal (pseudonym), said to me that she likes to use her walker for better stability and increased mobility; however, she feels that transporting the walker in her friends' vehicles is a burden, so she usually won't take it along. I find this sad because she really needs it to physically support herself.

I answered her: Opal, if you really want to know what being a burden feels like, what you do is use a wheelchair and try to board a city transit bus. Most of the drivers will despise you (but, happily, there are some who are very kind and professional and see it as part of their job!).

First, which is very time-consuming, the driver lowers a ramp so the wheelchair can be rolled up (in my case: pushed by my personal care attendant) and onto the bus. Then the driver pulls up a couple of seats, the benches at the front on one side of the bus. Then the wheelchair is rolled into place and turned, facing forward. Then the driver has to hook up both back sides with straps and then both front sides in the same way.

As the wheelchair person is leaving, everything is done in reverse. All the while, the other passengers are staring at you, frowning, and sending out negative, hate-filled vibes, because you are causing a delay in the schedule.

Maybe I left something out.

Anyway, try that some time. It's lots of fun.

12

Catholics and Protestants

The religiously devout are more hopeful and religion also provides adherents with a sense of purpose and meaning in life. Many religions teach that existence is not merely a random act of chance but rather the design of a creator who has purpose and intention and who desires human involvement in that purpose.[1]

When I was in my late thirties I became a Catholic and joined the parish of a Roman Catholic church. That is still a big part of my psychological make-up. Currently, I find some of my theological support through the homilies (sermons) and speeches given by an American prelate of the Catholic church, Bishop Robert Emmet Barron, whom I can view on-line. I disagree with some of his ideas but, generally, like much of what he says. Another person I listen to is the Catholic apologist and writer, Trenton Horn. I also listen to some who are Protestant. One, who passed away in 2023, is Timothy J. Keller, who was the founding pastor of Redeemer Presbyterian Church in New York City, co-founder of Redeemer City to City, and the author of several books. I really enjoy Tim Keller's teaching. There are others who might mention the teachings of John Calvin, Martin Luther, and some church fathers such as St.

1. Koenig et al., *Religion and Health*, 100.

Catholics and Protestants

Augustine. So, my beliefs are not purely Catholic or solely Protestant. I have found that both sides are rich in wisdom with much theological depth and that I cannot abandon one for the other. (I want to caution you, the reader, that there are some fake videos in the media created by AI and other such things that are distorting some of these public figures: you can't believe everything you see or hear. Go directly to the speaker's own website or organization to get the authentic materials.)

I know that some former Catholics left the church because they had conflict with priests. However, we should not throw out the baby with the bath water. Theologically, the Roman Catholic church's doctrine has much truth and goodness. Our relationship with Christ and his church is greater than any single relationship with a priest. Women who are victims of domestic violence may have been unjustly told to stick with their abusive spouse by a priest. This is, indeed, wrong. Priests can be wrong. But leaving an entire religious faith based on social things is probably extreme.

The Catholics and the Protestants need one another. Catholics seem to be rather methodical and what appears on the surface, rigid; and Protestants can often be too liberal and slack. What I mean by that is that with the Catholics you live by very strict rules. But with many Protestants there is the mindset that anything goes because God doesn't really care and will always give lots of grace and forgive. So we need to recognize that there are, indeed, boundaries and consequences which the Catholics are good at. Also, the Catholics are good at providing structure which is good for mental health. And as in Protestantism, God, who is patient, does give some grace and forgiveness. But we cannot be totally confined by rules or totally free. In living our daily lives we need to be able to see that some things are good and some things are bad; some things are true and some things are false. All Christians, both Catholic and Protestant need discernment with the wisdom to know how to live their lives. We can pray for wisdom.

13

Sidewalk

I WAS WALKING DOWN the sidewalk with my personal care attendant (who is also my friend), close to downtown, and near the University campus. Three adults, one male and two females, came in the direction toward us. They were spread out on the width of the sidewalk and when approaching me and my friend, they made absolutely no effort to fall into a formation that would allow people to pass on the side, to go in the opposite direction on the sidewalk. I was using my two forearm crutches and my friend fell in behind me. As those three people approached we had to step out onto the grass and stand there to let the people go by.

This is a gross example of extreme selfishness and discourtesy. Making a crippled person and her friend step off the concrete sidewalk to stand in the grass while they casually meandered by. What callousness and greed. The midwestern US has some who are not very Christian. The Christian way is to be considerate, kind, and generous. There are some mean-spirited human beings who are bullies.

14

Stronghold

> The Lord is a stronghold for the oppressed,
> a stronghold in times of trouble.
> And those who know thy name put their trust in thee,
> for thou, O Lord, hast not forsaken those who seek thee.
>
> (PSALM 9:9–10 RSV)

AN ACQUAINTANCE FROM THE joint areas of the psychiatric and spirituality academic sector requested that I share how I pray. So I will do so now.

My daily quiet time of prayer begins sometime between 12 midnight and 4am. This period of time is when it is quiet and I can have solitude. For my prayers, I put on a head garment that resembles a winter hat/scarf/shawl combination. The Bible says a woman should pray with her head covered (1Cor 11: 2–16 ESV). I feel much better this way and feel safe. I usually wear a hat, also, for Sunday morning worship services.

During my quiet time of prayer, I use a binder with papers in sheet protectors to hold the sections. I have a Catholic rosary and, also, an Anglican prayer beads. I use both consecutively and with the Catholic rosary, first. The Catholic rosary is used with my notebook of directions that contain my personal adaptations from the Roman Catholic rosary.[1] I use the Anglican prayer beads afterwards and they are without directions, prayers are said freely as I wish.

The steps I take when praying with my Catholic rosary:

1. Make the Sign of the Cross: In the name of the Father, Son, and Holy Spirit.

2. Say the Jesus prayer: Lord Jesus Christ, Son of God, have mercy on me, a sinner.

3. Say the *Our Father*

   Our Father, who art in heaven,
   hallowed be thy name;
   thy kingdom come;
   thy will be done;
   on earth as it is in heaven.
   Give us this day our daily bread.
   And forgive us our trespasses,
   as we forgive those who trespass against us.
   And lead us not into temptation;
   but deliver us from evil.
   For thine is the kingdom,
   the power and the glory,
   for ever and ever.
   Amen.[2]

4. Holding the Crucifix, say the *Apostles' Creed*.

   I believe in God, the Father Almighty,
   Maker of heaven and earth,
   And in Jesus Christ, His only Son, our Lord,
   who was conceived of the Holy Spirit,
   born of the Virgin Mary,

---

1. USCCB, https://www.usccb.org/how-to-pray-the-rosary.
2. Reformed Church, *Lord's Prayer,* para 2.

suffered under Pontius Pilate,
was crucified, died, and was buried.
He descended into hell.
On the third day He arose again from the dead.
He ascended into heaven
and sitteth at the right hand of God the Father Almighty,
from whence He shall come to judge the living and the dead.
I believe in the Holy Spirit,
the holy catholic church,
the communion of saints,
the forgiveness of sins,
the resurrection of the body,
and the life everlasting.
Amen.[3]

5. Say the Nicene Creed

We believe in one God, the Father, the Almighty, maker of heaven and earth, of all that is, seen and unseen.

We believe in one Lord, Jesus Christ, the only Son of God, eternally begotten of the Father, God from God, Light from Light, true God from true God, begotten, not made, of one being with the Father. Through him all things were made. For us and for our salvation, he came down from heaven, was incarnate of the Holy Spirit and the virgin Mary, and became fully human. For our sake he was crucified under Pontius Pilate. He suffered death and was buried. On the third day he rose again in accordance with the Scriptures. He ascended into heaven and is seated at the right hand of the Father. He will come again in glory to judge the living and the dead, and his kingdom will have no end.

We believe in the Holy Spirit, the Lord, the giver of life, who proceeds from the Father and the Son, who in unity with the Father and the Son is worshiped and glorified, who has spoken through the prophets. We believe in

---

3. Westminster, *Apostles Creed*, 1.

Faith and Major Mental Illness

one holy Christian and apostolic Church. We acknowledge one baptism for the forgiveness of sins.

We look for the resurrection of the dead and the life of the world to come. Amen.⁴

6. I finger each of the next three beads and thank God for the blessed Virgin Mary, for her obedience and humility.

7. Say the *Glory Be*

> *Glory be to the Father*
> *and to the Son*
> *and to the Holy Spirit,*
> *as it was in the beginning*
> *is now, and ever shall be*
> *world without end. Amen.*⁵

8. Different sections with topics depending on the day of the week, (perhaps followed by a brief reading from Scripture), [My personal topic adaptation from the Catholic rosary for my prayer beads.⁶] then say the *Our Father*.

9. 1ˢᵗ decade: *Joyful*

    Humility
    Love of Neighbor
    Poverty
    Purity of Heart and Body
    Devotion to Jesus

2nd decade: *Sorrowful*

    Obedience to God's will
    Mortification
    Courage
    Patience
    Sorrow for our sins

---

4. Marquette, *Nicene Creed*, 1.
5. USCCB, *How to Pray*.
6. USCCB, *How to Pray*.

3rd decade: *Glorious*

Faith
Hope
Wisdom

4th decade: *Luminous*

Openness to the Holy Spirit
Jesus and Mary
Conversion
Desire for Holiness
Adoration

10. Then say the *Glory Be*.

After finishing each section say the following prayer:

> O my Jesus, forgive us our sins, save us from the fires of hell; lead all souls to Heaven, especially those who have most need of your mercy.[7]

Ending with the sign of the cross: In the name of the Father, Son, and Holy Spirit.

After I've completed the use of this first rosary, I switch to the Anglican beads saying prayers of my own choosing. I begin by praising and thanking God. I repent for sins of commission and of omission. I ask God to expel all evil from within me and to fill me with the Holy Spirit. I request protection from all evil with a spiritual shield around me. I pray intercession for others, for those close to me, church friends, neighbors, and strangers. I thank God for a new day of life; and give thanks for all God has provided.

I pray for God's intervention in my life and for truth, love, and justice to prevail in the world. I ask for God's guidance, healing, and strength. I ask for help in all areas of my life. I ask for the ability to love God with my whole heart, mind, soul, and strength, and to love my neighbor as myself. I pray for my enemies, asking

---

7. USCCB, *How to Pray*.

God to bless them; and for the ability to forgive those who persecute me. I pray for the church leaders, the leaders in the medical field, and the civic leaders. I pray for the bus drivers, the librarians, and the employees who work in stores that my friend and I go to. I pray for the homeless and hungry, that they can get what they need. I pray for intervention in my country and the world where there is oppression and violence. I pray for peace.

Early in my prayer I pray for those closest to me, that God will protect them from harm, and that we can be healed. I ask for good health in body, mind, and spirit. I ask for grace, faith, hope, and love. Since my neighbors and I are imperfect, I ask that we can forgive one another and love each other. That we can have grace in our relationships. I ask for wisdom and clear direction. I ask God for a teachable heart and mind—to be transformed and made new.

I ask God for a servant's heart, humility, and that glory will go to him.

In the name of the Father, Son, and Holy Spirit. Amen.

I do not pray or do devotions the same way or at the same time of night or day. I usually read the Bible first for different lengths of time to begin devotions. I say my prayers as I am able, some prayers are longer than others. I also try to thank God at meals and before bedtime. I may also say short prayers, especially in times of need or anxiety and for strength.

Following, are some examples of other people's prayer experience that I have found helpful. In order to strengthen my own belief in the efficacy of prayer I see what others think and feel about things. I asked some people from my religious community if they wanted to answer my survey.

One participant responded:

My daily prayer issues pertain to healing, guidance, protection, strength, and often will include justice. Of course, many of my prayers veer from these topics.

Healing: I pray for others who I know are ill, struggling with pain, or who are afraid of something either physical or mental. I occasionally learn of the answers, and even if my prayers don't change the outcome it offers hope and a sense that someone cares, when others know I have prayed for them.

Guidance: I ask for guidance for myself and often for my children or grandchildren. I often need help with knowing the right road to take in certain instances. I have the satisfaction of feeling the guiding hand of God more often than not. It fills me with pleasure and a sense that I've been heard.

Protection: When traveling I always pray for travel mercies and when any of my family is starting on a long trip, I pray for their safety. Each day when I awaken I thank God for giving me protection and life for another day.

Strength: One of my most frequent prayers is for strength. I often feel unsure, afraid, or weak, and I know I can ask God to provide. When any trying situation is finished, I know my prayers were answered because I endured and maybe even thrived. God is good!

Justice: When I realize someone or something has been treated unfairly, I ask that justice be done. Sometimes I learn the outcome and at other times I don't. Usually, these are smaller things where I can intervene and talk to someone, but often I cannot. It requires a faith in the process and occasionally, the process doesn't work the way I want it to.

She continued: I'm way too human, so when I feel satisfied that my prayer was answered, I feel a bit smug, very pleased, and know that God heard my prayer. When I don't know whether my prayer was answered, or if it feels like it was, "no," I confess I was probably trying to tell God what to do and that has never worked! I try patience and have no trouble repeating my prayer request. Always, when I realize I've had an answer it strengthens my faith. However, when I realize I haven't had an answer or had a "no" answer, it doesn't necessarily diminish my faith, but makes me try harder and dig deeper, and perhaps change my prayer request.

One participant said that she will pray that if it is God's will for God to provide guidance and understanding. Another person, Patti, said that she mostly prays for a sense of reassurance, relief of anxiety, and support from a loving, listening ear (God). A person said that she prays for justice for people, especially, the oppressed, and justice which includes the environmental, financial, housing, food, and more. She said justice is slow and sometimes comes in legal or governmental wins, like bills passed. When she sees answers to prayers she rejoices in her heart that just decisions were made to benefit the oppressed.

> Religious involvement may promote certain behaviors or attitudes that increase happiness, satisfaction, and general well-being. Numerous studies have shown that religious persons are less likely to divorce or separate and are more likely to have intact, stable families.[8] Persons with high religious involvement are less likely to abuse alcohol and drugs; experience less hypertension, heart disease, stroke, cancer . . . and live longer.[9]
>
> There is greater social support. Religious institutions typically promote and even prescribe socialization among members of the congregation ("love they neighbor as thyself" Matt 22:39b RSV).[10]
>
> Many religious beliefs promote optimism and positive thinking.[11]

I believe it is helpful to see how others relate to God and how they feel about that relationship. The reason I feel this is helpful is because when I see the examples of others, it strengthens my own faith. I can't explain why, however. While everyone's faith is deeply individual and personal, there are some who are willing to share their thoughts. The following examples are provided by some individuals who answered my survey. The first one is from Rebecca, a scientist by education (PhD, Immunology) and profession (MD), while also a wife, and parent. She is a good example of a scientist who also has faith in God.

---

8. Koenig et al., *Religion and Health*, 99
9. Koenig et al., *Religion and Health*, 99.
10. Koenig et al., *Religion and Health*, 100.
11. Koenig et al., *Religion and Health*, 100.

GENERAL BELIEF

Marcia: Do you believe in a higher power or God?

Rebecca: Yes.

Marcia: How would you describe your current understanding of God?

Rebecca: Creator, sustainer who also made creation for his delight and our delight.

Marcia: How confident are you in your faith?

Rebecca: Very.

PRAYER PRACTICE

Marcia: How often do you pray?

Rebecca: Before meals and at various times short prayers.

Marcia: Do you pray in times of need only or throughout the day?

Rebecca: Mostly at times of need and delight.

Marcia: Do you feel comfortable expressing your thoughts and feelings openly in prayer?

Rebecca: Yes.

BIBLE STUDY/RELIGIOUS TEXT ENGAGEMENT:

Marcia: How often do you read religious texts?

Rebecca: Several times a week.

Marcia: Do you find meaning and guidance in your religious texts?

Rebecca: Yes.

Marcia: Do you actively study and reflect on the teachings within your religious texts?

Rebecca: Yes, I appreciate the *Bible Project Study Guide*.[12]

---

12. https://bibleproject.com/

Faith and Major Mental Illness

PERSONAL CONNECTION

Marcia: Do you feel a sense of personal connection with God?

Rebecca: Yes.

Marcia: Do you feel God's presence in your life?

Rebecca: Yes.

Marcia: How do you experience God's love?

Rebecca: In feelings of peace and joy that transcend whatever is going on. In receiving and giving love to others and the world around me.

GUIDANCE AND SUPPORT:

Marcia: When facing challenges, do you seek guidance from God?

Rebecca: Yes, especially for major decision or when I'm struggling with a specific issue.

Marcia: Do you feel comforted by God's presence during difficult times?

Rebecca: Yes, understanding that God will guide me and bring my worries to resolution.

Marcia: How do you make decisions that align with your faith?

Rebecca: Prayer, listening, discussion with others. Thinking about what I'm being called to do.

IMPACT ON LIFE:

Marcia: How does your faith influence your daily actions and choices?

Rebecca: It is the foundation of how I decide what is important and what God is doing in my life.

Marcia: Do you feel your faith motivates you to be a better person?

Rebecca: Yes.

Marcia: How does your faith shape your values and priorities?

Rebecca: Challenges me to be patient and wait, listen, hear God's voice in church, the Bible, and in prayer. [End of Rebecca]

    Other people shared their thoughts as well regarding their relationship with God. When asked do you believe in a higher power or God, many answered, yes, and described their current understanding as: everlasting creator, and redeemer. Another said that she feels confident of God's presence in her life. When asked about how often they pray, several said: daily. And they feel usually comfortable expressing their thoughts and feelings openly in prayer.

    When asked how often do you read religious texts, some said, daily, and others said frequently, not every day. As far as finding meaning and guidance in your religious texts, they all said, yes. When asked if they actively study and reflect on the teachings within your religious texts, they replied that they often do. All people who responded to my survey said that they feel a sense of personal connection with God and feel God's presence. When asked how they experience God's love, several said in an awareness of his presence through other people, nature, and music. When asked how they make decisions that align with their faith, they said that they bring them to God in prayer and read the Bible; and another said she reads scripture and connects with faithful people in her life.

    When asked how does their faith influence their daily actions and choices, one person said that her faith is a part of who she is and as a result helps guide her. Another said that she tries to live daily with God and follow with her actions. When asked if they feel their faith motivates them to be better people one responded that she believes we are all flawed individuals and she doesn't think of herself as better or worse. She does try to be aware of those around her and meet the needs of others as she is able. Another respondent remarked that she tries to live so that others can see Jesus in her.

As far as their faith shaping their values and priorities, one remarked that she feels like God is present with her and having grown up in a Christian home, she feels this shaped her from her youth. And as she has grown in her relationship with God, it continues to guide her values and priorities. Another person said that faith is at the center of all she does.

15

Resting in God

> I would love to just get to be able to do
> everything that I want,
> with no restrictions.

THE ULTIMATE REBELLION AGAINST God's authority: *Doing anything I want, all the time.*

As children, we desire to do anything we want to. That is why wise parents set up boundaries and rules, to guide them. A metaphorical example would be: you are walking down a sidewalk with your three-year-old next to a busy street full of traffic. As a liberal parent, you really don't want to tell your child what to do or think—after all, they should be *free*!! However, as soon as the child walks in the direction of the traffic, you decide to stop them and shout: *"Wait! Don't go there!"* So the liberal parent begins to understand that, indeed, a child needs guidance, not only physically, to stay out of danger, but morally, and theologically, too. But some parents never cross over into the moral or theological training of the child and as a result, the budding teen or young adult is thrown to the dogs of the secular culture, never to emerge again except by God's grace and provision. But they do not emerge unscathed. There are consequences.

Back in 2004 I attended a Presbyterian Health, Education, and Welfare Association (PHEWA) conference, put on by the Presbyterian Church (USA) down in Arizona. In this I met people from all over the country who felt justice issues mattered. One day in the hotel's restaurant, a senior gentleman asked if he could join me for lunch as I sat at a table. I consented and we held a lively discussion. He was a pastor emeritus at the doctorate level and wanted to know all about me. After learning I was a writer and published author, he made a request: *I want you to write something, a book, perhaps, in such a way as to bring together the Left and the Right in the church, the liberals, and conservatives. Do something with your writing that will help us get along and see the value in one another, regardless of our points of view. I know it won't be easy.*

I've been thinking about this sporadically for about twenty years. I've made a few attempts, but nothing major. Perhaps you, the reader, will see some value in this book you are reading in that regard. As a writer who has sympathy for both sides of the fence, I can say there is good on both sides. As far as the LGBTQ crowd there are some in this group who are very intelligent and certainly, kind. Though I disagree with their perspective on sexuality (and I have a right to my opinion), we certainly have some other things in common: love of life, love of family and love of neighbor. Love of God. After all, there is only one God who will judge the living and the dead. Our job is to try to get along, build each other up, and help one another.

On another matter, something I find disturbing is that currently there is a movement of conservatives that are denouncing the value of empathy, saying don't provide aid to others who are struggling. I feel this is wrong and that it's better to err on the side of kindness than to err on the side of cruelty. There are people who call themselves conservative Christians who criticize the acts of empathic compassion. I think they have taken this movement too far and the motivation is out of selfishness i.e., more for them, less for you, type of thinking. We can make too many judgments about the poor and oppressed based on ignorance and false information, and yes—selfishness. Greed. When I see acts of compassion, it makes me feel good. When I witness cruelty, I get depressed. Digging deeper into the causes of poverty and other types of misfortune takes time and most people would rather just watch television than find solutions.

When we deny people their basic human rights, this is going too far. Jesus Christ would not do this. The Christian way is to see to it that all are fed, clothed, and have shelter. Also, basic healthcare and legal defense in a court of law. When people have their basis needs taken care of, then we can sort out the psychological problems. We can work on emotional and behavior issues, mental health. But until people have their basic physical needs met we cannot work on the psychological issues.

So, I would disagree with these ultra-right conservatives. I say, do not judge—at least so harshly. Sure, some people have flaws and personality problems contributing to poverty, but let's sit down and talk with them, hear their stories, not shove them into jail cells where they deteriorate and rot away into oblivion, where there really is no hope for change. A compassionate Christian will offer hope which includes a hot meal, a shower, and clean change of clothes; somewhere to sleep and store belongings safely, so they can hold down a job; given decent wages so they can support themselves and loved ones above the poverty, subsistence levels. But this all takes patience, time, and effort, something many conservatives will not provide. They want a quick fix, always, the quick fix, and this is the violent, brutal way. Not God's way. God is patient, God has patience, and his ways take time. People who are patient and supportive of others reflect Christ, not those who destroy those who need assistance.

The acts of depriving the poor their basic rights are acts of violence, violence against humanity. Jesus Christ would never have done that. He lived to give good news to the poor, not incarcerate them all. Not condemn the poor. The biblical Gospels are full of stories and verses that show wealth can hinder us from Heaven. Jesus calls us to give away our riches and to follow him. Where our hearts are, where we put our treasure, this is what we value most in life (Matt 6:21 RSV).

Previously, I described a formality in the way I pray. But sometimes, I'm so weak I can only lie in my bed and repeat the words: *Jesus, help us, Jesus, please help us. Have mercy on us. Oh, God, have mercy on our souls.* I'm not the strongest person. My body is broken, my mind is not always focused. I stray in my heart. I still battle idols. And I certainly don't have all the answers. I look up to those who speak the truth. I've heard it said that our sin keeps up from hearing God's word in a church service. However, this presupposes that the preaching is actually the word of God. Sometimes, it is not. I've heard blasphemy and heresy preached in church. We are not totally safe. We need discernment and the strength to study our Bibles.

Sometimes a religious organization becomes a cult of personalities: elevating the pastor and the staff as though they are movie stars. We need to focus on Jesus Christ not the pastor. If we focus too much on the pastor, it becomes a cult. The pastor has the role to preach the word of God that points only to Jesus Christ, not him/or herself.

Ladies, you may not want to hear this, but men really are special in God's eyes. Sure, there is the occasional Debra the Judge, or Joan of Arc, but overall, men have a special role. We women need to look up to them in a way that shows respect. Men, overall, have greater strength; they need this especially because we are in a spiritual battle and are at war. We are fighting against all that tries to prevent us from loving and worshiping God. I am not a feminist but I am an advocate for equal respect between the genders, with kind regard for one another. But both men and women have different kinds of strengths and responsibilities. My authorities in Christian teaching have been and continue to be males. Right now, the Catholics provide the greatest theological guidance for me. Maybe in the future things might change, I cannot predict.

We are at war and the stakes are high. Our eternal lives will be determined by the choices we make here during our lifetimes. Problems of complacency are rampant. Diversions are everywhere:

sports, entertainment, wealth, or possessions/materialism. There are many things that get in the way of pure devotion to Christ. But as St. Augustine said: Nothing will satisfy us except being home with God. Our hearts need to focus on God. We are always restless, looking to the next thing, then the next.

> ... *for Thou has formed us for Thyself, and our hearts are restless till they find rest in Thee.*[1]

I described in this book which things make me feel alive. I shared my condition and life history, deadness, and, thank goodness, remedies. Christ is the healer. As a person who has struggled with major mental illness, I have found that any other way in life leads to a dead end. I am extreme, I know. I am radical and simple-minded, yes. But that is the way it is for me; and if you look around, also for many others. Hear their stories, feel their pain. Support them with compassion. Make room for them in your places of worship and gathering. Talk to them. Include them.

---

1. Augustine, *Confessions* 1.1.5.

APPENDIX

Further Reading

BOOKS BY MARCIA A. MURPHY
Founder, Mental Health Initiatives
Group for the Advancement of Mental Health

Concerning the Importance of God for Mental Health:Religious Faith and Its Relationship to Long-Term Cognitive, Emotional, and Behavioral Outcomes. Eugene: Resource Publications, 2025.
Author's book webpage: Concerning the Importance of God for Mental Health
Knitting with Barbed Wire: Understanding the Factor of Religion in Mental Illness & Health. Eugene: Resource Publications, 2024.
Author's book webpage: Knitting with Barbed Wire: Understanding the Factor of Religion in Mental Illness and Health by Marcia A. Murphy
The Compassionate Psychiatrist: Redefining Mental Healthcare. Eugene: Resource Publications, 2024.
Author's book webpage: The Compassionate Psychiatrist by Marcia A. Murphy
Homeless: The Unbefriended Poor. Eugene: Resource Publications, 2023.
Author's book webpage: Homeless
Schizophrenia and Suicide: Finding Hope, Meaning, and Direction. Eugene: Resource Publications, 2023.
Author's book webpage: Schizophrenia & Suicide: Finding Hope, Meaning, and Direction by Marcia A. Murphy
A Small Handbook of Mental Health: Portal to a New Life. Eugene: Resource Publications, 2022.
Author's book webpage: Small Handbook of Mental Health
Reflections on the Meaning of Mental Integrity: Recovery from Serious Mental Illness. Eugene: Resource Publications, 2021.

Appendix

Author's book webpage: https://wipfandstock.com/9781666708899/reflections-on-the-meaning-of-mental-integrity/

The Collected Writings of Marcia A. Murphy: Christus Magnus Medicus Sanat (Christ, the Great Physician, Heals). Eugene: Resource Publications, 2020.
Author's book webpage: https://hopeforrecovery.com/collected-writings/

To Loose the Bonds of Injustice: The Plight of the Mentally Ill and What the Church Can Do. Eugene: Resource Publications, 2018.
Author's book webpage: https://www.hopeforrecovery.com/to-loose-the-bonds-of-injustice/

Allbooks Review International Editor's Choice Award for 2011 Finalist:

Voices in the Rain: Meaning in Psychosis. Cedar Rapids, IA: Eagle Book Bindery, 2010. Repr., Eugene: Wipf & Stock Publishers, 2018.
Author's book webpage: https://www.hopeforrecovery.com/voices-rain-meaning-psychosis/

Bibliography

Faith at Marquette. *Nicene Creed*. https://www.marquette.edu/faith/prayers-nicene.php.

James, Adrian. Foreword to the Second Edition to *Spirituality and Psychiatry*, edited by Christopher C. H. Cook and Andrew Powell, 2nd ed. Cambridge, UK: Cambridge University Press, 2022.

Koenig, Harold G., Michael F. McCullough, and David B. Larson, eds., *Handbook of Religion and Health*. New York: Oxford University Press, 2001.

Murphy, Marcia A. *Knitting with Barbed Wire:Understanding the Factor of Religion in Mental Illness and Health*. Eugene: Resource Publications, 2024.

Reformed Church of America. *Liturgy: The Lord's Prayer*. https://www.rca.org/liturgy/the-lords-prayer/.

Saint Augustine of Hippo. *The Confessions of St. Augustine*. Edited by Joseph Green Pilkington, translated by Joseph Green Pilkington. Black and Gold Library: Immortal Classics; CA: Boni & Liveright, 1927. University of California, digitized Dec. 21, 2007. https://hdl.handle.net/2027/uc1.$b224078?urlappend=%3Bseq=59%3Bownerid=9007199259985489-63.

Simms, Eva-Maria. "Intimacy and the Face of the Other: A Philosophical Study of Infant Institutionalization and Deprivation." *Emotion, Space and Society* 13 (2014) 80–86.

United States Conference of Catholic Bishops (USCCB). *How to Pray the Rosary*. https://www.usccb.org/how-to-pray-the-rosary.

Westminster Presbyterian Church. *Apostles Creed*. https://wpcbryan.org/what-we-believe/apostles-creed/.

www.ingramcontent.com/pod-product-compliance
Lightning Source LLC
Chambersburg PA
CBHW071753040426
42446CB00012B/2533